Prosperity Teachings
of the Bible
(Made Easy)

Prosperity Teachings of the Bible (Made Easy)

Maggy Whitehouse

AXIS MUNDI
BOOKS

Winchester, UK
Washington, USA

First published by Axis Mundi Books, 2012
Axis Mundi Books is an imprint of John Hunt Publishing Ltd., Laurel House, Station Approach,
Alresford, Hants, SO24 9JH, UK
office1@o-books.net
www.o-books.com

For distributor details and how to order please visit the 'Ordering' section on our website.

ISBN: 978 1 78099 107 8

A CIP catalogue record for this book is available from the British Library.

Design: Lee Nash

Printed in the United States by Edwards Brothers, Inc.

We operate a distinctive and ethical publishing philosophy in all
areas of our business, from our global network of authors to
production and worldwide distribution.

CONTENTS

Introduction

At first glance the Hebrew and New Testaments of the Bible would appear to be completely different on the subject of prosperity. The Hebrew teachings seem to encourage the accumulation of wealth while the Gospels and letters of the New Testament recommend discarding riches and living a simple life.

> *"Thou shalt remember the Lord thy God for it is He that giveth thee the power to get wealth."* **Deuteronomy 8:18**.

> *"I tell you it is easier for a camel to pass through the eye of a needle than for a rich man to enter into the kingdom of heaven."* **Gospel of Matthew 19:24**.

But is there more to it than that? Is there an underlying, unifying theme of what prosperity actually *is* and how to attract it throughout the whole of the Bible? I believe that there is and that this ancient text, interpreted carefully and comprehensibly, is a prosperity workbook for the modern age.

If you ask people what they want from life, most will say that they wish for themselves and their loved ones to be happy and healthy. Then they will add the desire for good relationships and enough money to live a comfortable life. Yes, there are those who seek fame and fortune, fast cars, big houses and millions in their bank accounts (and this is actively encouraged in the modern world). And why should people not have these things? Does the Bible say that we should not? Or does it just warn that the word "possession" has both an active and a passive meaning. Do we possess our goods or do they possess us?

From 20 years experience of studying and teaching the spiritual laws of prosperity, I believe that many people's issues over money come from misinterpretations of Biblical teachings and the commentaries on them by later teachers. Unless we look at these teachings through the social, economic and spiritual filters of the times when they were written, we cannot fully understand their initial intention.

We also need to look at what prosperity itself actually means. The root of the word "prosperity" dates back to the early 13th century from the Old French *prosperite* (c. 1140) from Latin *prosperitatem* (n) meaning "good fortune."

Webster's dictionary describes it as "the condition of being successful or thriving especially economic wellbeing." It defines the verb "to prosper" as "to succeed in an enterprise or activity, especially to achieve economic success" and "to become strong and flourishing."

It's only the money aspect of prosperity which seems to cause an issue within faiths. However, money is required in the modern world as the agent of exchange with which we humans operate. With money and leisure we have developed civilization.

The goal of this book is to help those who wish to work with Biblical texts to understand that it may be possible (and even desirable) to make peace with money and see it not as an evil thing but as the oil we humans have chosen to grease the wheels of life.

Hopefully this book will give you a clear outline of the teachings on prosperity that are evident throughout the Bible. However, please understand that these are my interpretations, based on Jewish and Christian mysticism. You may not agree with my findings but perhaps they will inspire you to take time to reconsider your own beliefs about money and spirituality.

Chapter One

Conventional Jewish and Christian views on money

It would be fair to suggest that, although the main cause of divergence between Judaism and Christianity is the issue of whether or not Jesus of Nazareth was the Messiah, financial issues have also been at the forefront of enmity between the two faiths for almost as long as Christianity has existed.

For centuries a general view of Judaism and Christianity that has pervaded Western thought is that Jews are money-oriented while Christians see hard work or even poverty as best representing religious faith. The Jewish nation believes that it is a virtue to prosper; that it is the Lord's intention that if they remember their faith and deal honestly, they will be rewarded:

> *"Through wisdom is a house builded; and by understanding it is established: And by knowledge shall the chambers be filled with all precious and pleasant riches."* **Proverbs 24:3-4**.

In contrast, the "Protestant Work Ethic" emphasizes the necessity for struggle as a part of a person's calling and the heroes and heroines of Catholicism are the saints and martyrs who denied themselves practically everything.

There is no doubt that, given the ratio of Christians to Jews in the world, the Jewish nation has had spectacular success in the business and media worlds. However, all too often the Christian view on Jewish people is that they are grasping or dishonest and that they deal with something distasteful in money. We only have to look at the story of Shylock in Shakespeare's *The Merchant of Venice* to see the level of prejudice that had built by the sixteenth century. Shylock says to Antonio:

"Many a time and oft,
In the Rialto you have rated me
About my moneys and my usances;
Still have I borne it with a patient shrug,
For suff'rance is the badge of all our tribe;
You call me misbeliever, cut-throat dog,
And spit upon my Jewish gaberdine,
And all for use of that which is mine own.
Well then, it now appears you need my help;
Go to, then; you come to me, and you say
'Shylock, we would have moneys.'"

Contrast this with the story of St. Francis of Assisi, one of Christianity's most loved saints and the son of a wealthy man who chose instead to embrace poverty. His Franciscan order of Monks was endorsed by the Pope in 1210; he also founded the Poor Clares, an enclosed order for women, and also a Third Order of Brothers and Sisters of Penance. All of these embraced a life of self-denial.

While modern Christians in an economically-driven world may no longer accept the idea of Franciscan-style poverty, there is still a belief among many Christians that it is somehow wrong to be religious and rich.

The Vatican

The incredible wealth of the Vatican is an issue for many especially as much of that wealth in earlier days was amassed through buying "indulgences," the full or partial remission of punishment for sins after the sinner has confessed and received absolution. These are still granted today within the Catholic Church in return for specific good works and prayers but, in the Middle Ages, they were often bought by the wealthy.

Supporters of the Vatican justify its wealth by saying that the vast majority of the Catholic Church's property (e.g. churches, schools and hospitals) is specifically dedicated to the service of people, especially the poor. In the case of art and property, the Church considers itself the guardian of treasures for the whole world, making them available for pilgrims and tourists to enjoy. It emphasizes that revenue obtained by displaying these items is then used to assist the needs of people everywhere.

The Church has always used gold and jewels for sacred vessels because it believes they hold the body and blood of Christ. This is following in the tradition of the wealth of the ancient Jewish Temple which was first built as a moving tabernacle during the time of the Exodus from Egypt, transformed into the magnificence of Solomon's Temple and then purged by King Josiah. It was made magnificent again in the time of Herod the Great (circa 73-4BCE) and destroyed by the Romans in 70CE, never to be rebuilt. Since then, the Jews have worshipped in Synagogues which are places of beauty but comparative modesty. The Vatican has become the Christian Catholic Temple so Judaism and Christianity have swapped roles in that respect.

The Bible and Money

The Bible contains approximately 2,350 references to money and how to handle it. In both Testaments, how wealth is managed is depicted as one of the important aspects of spiritual growth.

Certainly, from the start, Christians celebrated the virtues of poverty and chastity while the Jewish nation always believed in prosperity, marriage and reproduction. Jesus is popularly seen as a poor, itinerant preacher who gave healing for free and who taught that *"ye cannot serve both God and mammon."* **Matt. 6:24**. *Mammon* is an Aramaic word usually translated as money but Webster's dictionary defines it as "the false god of riches and avarice and as riches regarded as an object of worship and greedy pursuit; wealth as an evil, more or less personified."

3

The primary difficulty between Christian and Jewish views on money appears to be this interpretation. Is money a neutral energy imbued with the energy of the people handling it or is it, itself, a source of idolatry and evil?

Although some of Jesus' teachings on wealth are well known, just as many of Christianity's views about finance come from or through St. Paul and his followers. It is useful to realize from the start that Jesus was a Jew who came from provincial Galilee where barter was the main form of commerce and few possessions were needed. Paul, on the other hand, was a Roman citizen, spreading the message across the cities and centers of finance across the Empire where possessions proclaimed wealth and power.

Galilee was regarded as very unsophisticated by those living in Jerusalem in Jesus' day. The country people, however, saw those in the cities being corrupted by Roman lifestyles and morals and almost certainly despaired at their children's desire to investigate the new, the shining and the exotic. No matter how the orthodox resisted the attractions of the new—and hated—regime, Roman Jerusalem was doing the equivalent of offering Pepsi and McDonalds to a new generation that wanted to be cool.

After the destruction of the Temple in 70CE, Jews scattered throughout the world and by the time that the *Mishnah* and *Talmud* (written commentaries and instruction on the *Torah*) were finally crystallized and written down between 200 and 400CE, the Jewish culture was more urban than agricultural. However, it still remained very self-contained, honoring teachings from centuries beforehand. Christianity, however, was deeply affected by Roman attitudes towards money and lending, especially after the new religion was formally adopted by the Emperor Constantine in 313CE.

Usury

In the Roman Empire, banking activities and money lending were conducted by private individuals, not by companies.

Anybody who wished to lend money could charge whatever rate of interest they liked. There were no legal limits on interest and, although this was usually between four and 12 per cent, it could go as high as 24 per cent or 48 per cent.

It was this principal of lending at interest—known as *usury*—which became the primary financial issue between Judaism and Christianity—and later on for Islam also.

The root of the matter comes from **Deuteronomy 23:10-21** which prohibits usury for "brothers" but permits it for "foreigners." Jews therefore would lend money at interest to non-Jews but without interest to each other. Early Christians may well have followed the same idea, regarding other Christians as their "brothers." However, as the followers of the faith became more and more Romanized, they lent money at interest too. That is, until the fourth century, when the First Council of Nicaea in 325 (canon 17) forbade the clergy to lend money on interest above one percent per month (12.7% APR).

The Third Council of the Lateran in 1179 took this further, ruling that any Christians charging interest on loans could receive neither the sacraments nor a Christian burial. In 1311, Pope Clement V made usury a heresy, resulting in excommunication and possibly even execution, and abolished all secular legislation that had allowed it.

As the Jewish nation was, by then, a marginalized minority that was prevented by law from practicing many trades throughout Europe, the Jews were increasingly allowed only to carry out the work considered socially inferior, such as tax and rent collecting, peddling and money lending.

Natural tensions between creditors and debtors added to social, political, religious and economic strains and, if Jews trying to make a living reacted by concentrating on money lending to non-Jews, their unpopularity increased.

Protestantism, Islam and Usury

Despite the prohibitions of usury by Popes and civil legislators, loopholes in the law kept being found and, along with the growing tide of commercialization, a Christian pro-usury counter-movement began to grow. The arrival of Protestantism brought more financial tolerance for, although both Luther and Calvin expressed reservations about the practice of usury, they didn't believe that it should be condemned out of hand. Usury became simply a matter of private conscience and a new generation of Christian moralists redefined the term as "excessive interest" in the early 1620s.

This left Islam as the only one of the three faiths descended from the Hebrew Bible to condemn money-lending at interest outright. Orthodox Islam is as emphatic today as orthodox Christianity was in the 11th century.

The Koran says:

"Those who charge usury are in the same position as those controlled by the devil's influence. This is because they claim that usury is the same as commerce. However, God permits commerce, and prohibits usury. Thus, whoever heeds this commandment from his Lord, and refrains from usury, he may keep his past earnings, and his judgment rests with God. As for those who persist in usury, they incur Hell, wherein they abide forever." (**Al-Baqarah 2:275**).

In modern day Islam the orthodox work only with those banks who do not charge interest and there are specific rules in place over issues such as mortgages. For example, if a Muslim wants to buy a house but does not have the full amount, he or she will enter into a financial partnership with a company and then rent the property from the main funder of the purchase. To some observers the end result appears to be the same as lending but no interest is charged.

Non-orthodox Muslims, together with Christians and Jews, have adopted the current economic view that interest is perfectly acceptable.

Chapter Two

New Thought Churches

What much of the secular world considers to be the prosperity teachings of the Bible became popular between the end of the 19th century and the 1940s with the advent of what became known as New Thought Churches. These inspired a movement of positive thinking and the work of multi-million-selling speakers and writers such as Norman Vincent Peale, Napoleon Hill and Florence Scovel Shinn. They can also be seen as the precursor to the 21st century phenomena of Rhonda Byrne's *The Secret*, (Simon & Schuster), Barbel Mohr's *Cosmic Ordering Service* (Mobius) and the work of Louise L. Hay and Esther and Jerry Hicks.

New Thought began teaching that it is humanity's right—and even duty—to live a prosperous life. This prosperity included physical healing and financial comfort, if not outright wealth. While late 20th and 21st century interpretations of these teachings nowadays are often used by gurus who promise that you can make millions from the techniques, the original intention within the New Thought movement was to help Christian people out of grinding poverty and bring healing to diseases deemed incurable before the advent of modern medicine.

New Thought Churches use the Bible (particularly the New Testament) to demonstrate that both physical sickness and financial poverty are consequences of erroneous beliefs and that our thoughts and emotions have physical results in our bodies. They teach that a mind open to God's wisdom can overcome any illness. There is an emphasis on understanding the difference between being "to blame" for finding ourselves in a given situation and in being "responsible" for it.

In New Thought, responsibility for poverty or sickness is defined as how we have responded to outside circumstances (response-ability). The movement teaches that being unhappy, angry, frustrated and throwing blame at others for how we feel cuts off our contact with Divine abundance and love.

New Thought Women

New Thought promotes affirmative statements from the Bible and positive interpretations of both Old and New Testaments to demonstrate that clear thinking can change lives. Many of the original church leaders did receive miracle cures from sicknesses which had been diagnosed as be incurable. Myrtle Fillmore, co-founder of *Unity*, was a mother of three who had a terminal diagnosis of tuberculosis. She refused to accept this death sentence and began to investigate alternatives, attending a lecture with a student of one of the originators of New Thought, Emma Curtis Hopkins. Myrtle came out of the meeting convinced that her mind could heal her body, threw away all her medicines and decided to believe that she was already healthy, despite her poor physical condition. In the months to follow she was totally healed and lived to the age of 86 with a powerful healing ministry of her own.

Many of the early church founders of the New Thought movement were women including Mary Baker Eddy, Emma Curtis Hopkins, Myrtle Fillmore, Malinda Cramer and Nona. L. Brooks. Frequently, its churches and community centers were led by women, from the 1880s to the present day. New Thought Churches were, then, the only places where women could preach as teachers and ministers within a form of Christianity.

Where the women generally focused on healing, teaching that there was a science behind the healing miracles of Jesus which could be practiced by anyone, the men within the movement are better known for their teaching on financial prosperity—the exception being *Unity*'s Catherine Ponder, author of the million-selling *Dynamic Laws of Prosperity* and the *Millionaires of the Bible* series.

Both Charles Fillmore and Catherine Ponder, from *Unity*, describe poverty as a "sin," saying that it is contrary to God's desire for us. However, despite the fact that "sin" is defined in all their books as being an archery term for "missing the mark" rather than a wicked act, *Unity* nowadays prefers to take a softer approach.

In *Prosperity* (Unity House), Charles Fillmore writes:

"We cannot be happy if we are poor and nobody needs to be poor. It is a sin to be poor. You may ask whether Jesus cited any example of poverty's being a sin? Yes. You will find it in the story of the Prodigal Son."

In this parable, the son of a wealthy man takes his inheritance and squanders it in wild living. He is reduced to penury but, after much suffering, realizes that if he returns to his father's house with a humble heart, ready to serve, he will be better off than he is now. At the end of the story, his father welcomes him home with joy and rewards him.

Scriptural Interpretation

Like much New Thought teaching, Charles Fillmore's work demonstrates a positive interpretation of Scripture which may not be strictly literal. This is his "prosperity treatment" of the 23rd Psalm:

"The Lord is my banker; my credit is good.
He maketh me to lie down in the consciousness of omnipresent
*   abundance.*
He giveth me the key to His strongbox.
He restoreth my faith in His riches;
He guideth me in the paths of prosperity for His name's sake.

Yea, though I walk in the very shadow of debt,
I shall fear no evil, for Thou art with me;
Thy silver and Thy gold, they secure me.
Thou preparest a way for me in the presence of the collector;
Thou fillest my wallet with plenty; my measure runneth over.
Surely goodness and plenty will follow me all the days of my life,
And I shall do business in the name of the Lord forever."

Florence Scovel Shinn (1871-1940), author of *The Game of Life and How to Play It* (De Vorss), was an inspiration to many New Thought Churches and teachers and used many Biblical phrases and texts. Florence's philosophy was that invisible forces are always working for humanity and that, due to the vibratory power of words, whatever we voice, we begin to attract. In *The Game of Life*, she quotes **Proverbs 18:21**, *"life and death are in the power of the tongue"* and **Matthew 12:37**, *"By thy words thou shalt be justified and by thy words thou shalt be condemned."*

In *The Secret Door to Success* (De Vorss) Florence wrote, *"'According to your faith be it unto you,'* **(Matt. 9:29)**. Faith is expectancy. We might say, according to your expectancies be it done unto you. So what are you expecting? We hear people say 'We expect the worst to happen' or 'the worst is yet to come.' They are deliberately inviting the worst to come."

In *The Millionaire from Nazareth* (De Vorss), Catherine Ponder updates the Beatitudes from the Gospel of Matthew **(5:3-7)**. She reinterprets the fourth Beatitude, *"Blessed are they that hunger and thirst after righteousness: for they shall be filled,"* as, "Those who hunger and thirst after the right use of prosperous ideas shall find their lives filled with abundant blessings."

Catherine translates the sixth Beatitude, *"Blessed are the pure in heart for they shall see God"* into "Blessed are the pure in heart who always picture success for each experience. Through picturing God's goodness they shall experience the peace, health and plenty of true abundance."

Mystics come to us in every generation to interpret Scripture for the modern age and there is no doubt that New Thought has been the foundation of much spiritual prosperity consciousness throughout the world. It was termed "metaphysics" by many of the New Thought teachers. However, it has also attracted criticism for its innovative translations and has been seen, by some, as giving people unfounded hope.

However, for the most part, New Thought teachers simply interpret known Biblical sayings and demonstrate how they can be seen to bring prosperity at all levels. The emphasis is on a flow of all the goodness of the world including finances, rather than on the accumulation of huge wealth and possessions. *"The sole thought of money-getting is being allowed by men and women to generate its cold vapor in their souls until it shuts out all the sunlight of love and even of life,"* wrote Charles Fillmore in 1936. His own answer was to live in community with everything shared but he was aware that this was a difficult prospect for most people.

New Thought Churches

The best-known New Thought Churches include *Church of Religious Science, Christian Science, Unity* and *Church of Divine Science* although, in fact, *Christian Science* has far more fundamental beliefs than the others. Nearly all of the churches referred to "science" in their first teachings due to their views being new and radical at a time when the word was still linked with philosophy and radical thinking. Before the modern criterion of physical proof in the areas of physics, chemistry, biology and geology became the only scientific method, the original Latin word, *scientia*, meant "knowledge."

The Church of Divine Science was founded in San Francisco in the 1880s by Malinda Cramer and Nona Brooks. Nona defined the name as, *"The whole of Divine Science is the practice of the Presence of God. Truth comes through the Bible, affirmative prayer, contemplation and meditation and the practice of the presence of God here and now."*

Christian Science (full name, *The First Church of Christ, Scientist*) is based on the Bible and the writings of Mary Baker Eddy (1821-1910). In her *Science & Health With Key to the Scriptures,* Mrs. Eddy described the teachings and healings of Jesus as a complete and coherent science evident and provable through physical healing. Most New Thought Churches moved away from Mary's teachings as she was anti-medicine in any form and anti the material world as well. Generally, New Thought embraces medical science with the view that all healing is spiritual healing whether it is through the work of a surgeon or a drug or through prayer.

Unity, founded by Charles and Myrtle Fillmore, in Kansas City in 1914, identifies itself as "Christian New Thought," focused on "Christian idealism," with the Bible as one of its main texts. Charles and Myrtle studied the Bible as history and allegory and interpreted it as a metaphysical representation of humanity's evolutionary journey toward spiritual awakening. *Unity* believes that we are all part of "Divine Mind" and that Jesus expressed his full divinity and sought to show all humanity how to express its own divinity too. It uses the term *Christ* to mean the divinity in humankind. Jesus is seen as the great example of the Christ in expression.

Religious Science, also known as *Science of Mind,* was established in 1927 by Ernest Holmes (1887–1960). Holmes did not originally intend it to be a church, defining it as "a correlation of laws of science, opinions of philosophy, and revelations of religion applied to human needs and the aspirations of man." The three primary spiritual practices advocated by *Science of Mind* are: affirmative prayer, meditation, and visioning (visualization).

However, perhaps the best known of all positive thinkers was Norman Vincent Peale, author of *The Power of Positive Thinking.* Peale was a Protestant minister and pastor the Marble Collegiate

Church, a Reformed Church in America congregation in New York City, from the year 1932 to 1984. At the time of his retirement the church had 5,000 members and tourists lined up around the block to hear Peale preach. Peale's weekly radio program, *The Art of Living*, was broadcast on NBC for 54 years. His sermons were mailed to 750,000 people a month. His *Guidepost Magazine* continues its popularity today having a circulation of more than 4.5 million, the largest for any religious publication.

Peale acknowledged that his theology of positive thinking came from Ernest Holmes although the phrase "Positive Thinking" came originally from Charles Fillmore. However, it was Peale who made it popular world-wide.

Peale's view of the universe as God as an energy, and of prayer as the scientific technique for releasing God-energy according to definite laws. One of Peale's best-known quotations sums up the New Thought movement: *"Change your thoughts and you change the world."*

Chapter Three

The Prosperity Gospel

New Thought churches differ from the Prosperity Gospel teachings of the modern Evangelical churches in that their ministers have felt free to interpret the teachings of the Bible for everyone, encouraging their students to focus on the idea of the Christ consciousness within each human being and a universally-loving God. A New Thought teacher will explain how we can all use Jesus' teachings to find our own right path and make healthy choices as individuals.

The Prosperity Gospel movement also believes that it is God's wish for humanity to prosper and that it is our wrong thinking which blocks the way; and Prosperity Gospel preachers interpret the Bible in their own metaphysical way. The striking difference is the Prosperity Gospel's focus on fundamental Christianity — Jesus Christ is our only savior. If you are not born again, please don't apply!

The Prosperity Gospel is also known as Prosperity Doctrine, the Health and Wealth Gospel or Prosperity Theology. It became popular in the 1950s with teachers such as Oral Roberts and his *Expect a Miracle* TV evangelism. The idea that Jesus will bless believers with riches was a popular thought at a time when radio and television were telling Americans that greater comfort could be accessible to everyone. It thrived during the wealth-conscious 1990s and is now spreading across the Hispanic and African churches in the USA and the rest of the world. In December 2009 *Atlantic* magazine claimed that the Prosperity Gospel had "tens of millions" of adherents in the USA alone.

Oral Roberts

Here is a quotation from Oral Roberts (taken from www.ondoc-trine.com) which sums up the Prosperity Gospel teaching:

> *"Acts 3:1-10 tells the story of the healing of the lame man at the Beautiful Gate. He was carried to the gate of the temple each day, where he begged for a living. One day, as the apostles Peter and John were approaching the temple, they stopped before him. Verse five says the beggar looked up, 'expecting to receive' something from them—most likely coins. But Peter and John told him, 'We don't have any money, but such as we have we give to you.'*
>
> *"With those words, the beggar's expectancy changed. He no longer expected money. He expected what they could give him—the healing power of Jesus of Nazareth! They commanded him, 'In the name of Jesus Christ, rise up and walk!' And the man stood up and began walking and running into the temple, leaping and praising god. All because he expected to be healed!*
>
> *"To receive the miracle-working power of God it's important to be in a state of expectancy. Three things happen when you expect.*
>
> *"First, you recognize your miracle when it comes your way.*
>
> *"Second, you use your faith to reach out for your miracle.*
>
> *"And third, you receive it into your heart.*
>
> *"Right now, expect a miracle to happen, and it can happen!"*

It's a moot point whether the beggar was expecting a healing miracle; there's nothing actually to say that in the Gospel. There is no indication that he even knew Peter and John and their teacher. But Oral's interpretation is quite possible—and certainly attractive to those asking for healing.

The Prosperity Gospel teaches that God will always reward faith with health and wealth and, although it is completely Christian, it is comfortable with using Old Testament quotations such as **Malachi 3:10**, "*And prove me now herewith, saith the Lord of Hosts, if I will not open you the windows of heaven, and pour you out* *a blessing, that there shall not be room enough to receive it."*

Prosperity Gospel teaching is not a specific doctrine, rather a thread that runs through the Pentecostal church and many other evangelical groups. It has spread hugely through TV, radio and now Internet evangelism which promises that God will shower blessings on Christians in their lifetime. Of course, this is in sharp contrast to the more traditional Christian view that the faithful will receive their reward in heaven and that self-denial and even suffering are the road to glory.

Giving

Like many New Thought Churches, the Prosperity Gospel preachers emphasize giving to the ministry. This is often referred to as tithing, the giving of the first tenth of your income to support church, synagogue or temple. Tithing is a principle from the Hebrew Bible which will be discussed in detail in Chapter Four.

American preachers such as the appropriately-named Creflo Dollar, Joyce Meyer, Paul Couch and Kenneth Copeland encourage their followers to "sow seeds" of faith by donating money to the ministry in the understanding that God will repay them a hundredfold.

One of the texts that is used to encourage giving is St. Paul's first letter to the Corinthians, *"And now, brothers and sisters, we want you to know about the grace that God has given the Macedonian churches. In the midst of a very severe trial, their overflowing joy and their extreme poverty welled up in rich generosity. For I testify that they gave as much as they were able, and even beyond their ability. Entirely on their own, they urgently pleaded with us for the privilege of sharing in this service to the Lord's people. And they exceeded our expectations: They gave themselves first of all to the Lord, and then by the will of God also to us ... see that you also excel in this grace of giving. I am not commanding you, but I want to test the sincerity of your love by comparing it with the earnestness of others. For you know the grace of our Lord Jesus Christ, that though he was rich, yet for your sake he became poor, so that you through his poverty might become rich"* (**1 Cor. 8**)

This is a wonderful example of the subtle manipulation that can be used to encourage giving in any circumstances. Paul is not telling them they *have* to give; he just wants to know how sincere they are in their faith. There is also the strong implication that Jesus suffered for our sake. Any Christian who didn't give in such circumstances would most likely feel a great deal of guilt.

Followers of the Prosperity Gospel, like both New Thought believers and New Agers, use prosperity statements, known as *affirmations*, in order to align themselves to the Divine Substance which will bring them prosperity.

That this is comforting and helpful, I can confirm. At the time when my first husband was dying and we had no income, I knew nothing of any of the prosperity teachings but I affirmed to myself Jesus' saying, *"Consider the lilies of the field, how they grow; they neither toil nor spin, yet I tell you, even Solomon in all his glory was not arrayed like one of these."* (**Matt. 6:28-29**) which felt much more helpful than fretting all the time. A worried person is less likely to make clear decisions than a calm one so there is a logic behind affirmation as long as the person affirming can truly feel the good effect of the words.

Joel Olsteen

The largest church in America is a Prosperity Gospel one, Lakewood, in Texas. This has a 43,500-strong congregation, double the number of any other church in the USA. The pastor is Joel Olsteen. The church includes a financial ministry ten-week class series promising *"spiritual teachings and application tools that are life changing, spiritually fulfilling, fun, and financially relevant to empower you to eliminate debt, build wealth, discover the joy of giving, and follow biblical financial principles."*

This is what the Lakewood website, www.lakewood.cc, says about giving:

"Giving is a biblical principal that when lived by, produces a rich harvest in our lives. Giving is not limited to simply our finances; it's a lifestyle. When we live with the spirit of giving, when we give the Lord our tithes and our offerings, when we give to those in need, when we give of our time, our love, our resources, we are sowing seeds that God will make sure blossoms into a rich harvest! Not just of financial blessings, but rich in all aspects of life. He'll make sure the right doors open, the right people come into your life, and the right breaks are received.

"God desires for you to be the most blessed and most prosperous in the land, that we prosper in our homes, relationships and in health. Make sure you work with God and allow His door of favor and provision to open like a flood by putting actions to your faith through giving.

"And we don't give to simply receive. The important thing is that we live with the spirit of giving. God is more concerned with the condition of your heart as you give, rather than the quantity.

"It is through our giving where the greatest blessings and provision can be seen.

"Do you need a miracle in your life? A Breakthrough? A financial need? Try giving. God says, *'Test me in this. See if I will not throw open the floodgates of heaven and pour out so much blessings there will not be room enough to store it.'"* (**Malachi 3:10**).

The top ten churches in the USA all have a link on their home page for online donations. This is not, in itself, unusual—most churches in the world ask for gifts for funds for rebuilding or charity work but, with regular giving from congregations of 20,000, plus these are very wealthy establishments.

I once attended a UK talk by *Unity's* Catherine Ponder where she passed buckets round the auditorium urging the audience to give generously to her ministry in order to prosper themselves through God's response to our generosity. This was in addition to the fee already paid for attending the lecture and it certainly ruffled a few conventional British feathers.

Saying this is not intended to be a judgment against the ministers; it is simply not in line with what most people in less evangelical churches are taught is the norm. However, their very success indicates that their teachings bring great hope to their congregations.

The new good news is that God doesn't want us to wait; a God who loves you does not want you to be broke. The Prosperity Gospel signature verse could be **John 10:10**:

"I have come that they may have life, and that they may have it more abundantly."

It's an attractive belief but it comes with the rider that you must accept Jesus as your savior.

Chapter Four

Life and times in Biblical days

It's not easy to understand the Bible with a 21st century mind; we bring so many of our modern beliefs and projections to the contents. If we have learnt that God is cruel, we will see a cruel God; if we believe that God is good, we will justify or skip over any apparent opposition to that view. If we are Christian, we will read the Hebrew Testament through very different eyes from those of a Jew, an agnostic or an atheist. It is important to understand that we cannot remove ourselves and our beliefs from this sacred text. And if we have specific beliefs about money, wealthy people and authority, then we will be reading through those filters also.

It is also essential to realize that people in ancient times did not think the way we do. The people whose stories are being told did not comprehend our great cities with their rush-rush mentality. The population of Rome at its height was approximately one million people, about the same as 19th century London—then the largest city in the world. And Rome is not where the stories take place. They happen in mostly rural societies where the night sky was regarded with awe and fables were told to explain the purpose and the meaning of existence.

People in Biblical times did not experience the news in the way we do. Details of events from another part of the country—let alone another part of the world—could take weeks, months or years to arrive. There was no entertainment such as books to read. In fact, even in cosmopolitan Rome in Jesus' time, 95 per cent of the population could not read or write; if anyone needed to send a letter, they hired one of the five per cent, usually a professional scribe, and the recipient the other end would hire another scribe to read the letter to them.

Even those who could read text did not do so silently as we do; they read out loud so that others could share the information. The concept of reading quietly was unknown in Roman times or before. Roman villas even had private reading rooms where the literate could read out loud to themselves without disturbing the rest of the family. It was only in the time of St. Augustine (354-430) that we hear about the first silent reading being developed, perhaps, from the requirements of monastic life.

Without easy access to information, the only entertainment available once work had finished and supper was eaten was either music or stories. And the music generally involved stories. So a travelling storyteller or holy man with new tales, teachings or ideas would, most likely, have been a very welcome guest in a village. Of course, some of them might have been controversial and sent away with their tails between their legs but even that would be an event to be debated for months in places where very little other news occurred.

The work of the Scribes

This aspect of literacy is important in the discussion of Biblical wealth as Jewish religious teachings were preserved in sacred scrolls that were written by professional scribes. This is still the case for the Torah scrolls in any synagogue. Sacred work could not just be written out by anyone; it required an expert scribe to copy out the whole of the *Sefer Torah* (the first five books of the Hebrew Testament) where every version had to be perfect. It could take a scribe up to 18 months to complete one scroll, during which time he could earn no other living. Therefore, wealthy benefactors were required to pay for religious writings whether that payment was in kind or in silver or gold.

This applied to a certain extent in the Christian world in that benefactors gave money to monasteries, where monk-scribes would write out beautiful, illuminated copies of the Bible.

However this practice decreased dramatically with the invention of the printing press in the mid-15th century. Also, the Christian scribes were men who had made vows of poverty, chastity and obedience and lived in celibate communities. In the Jewish world the scribe, like the Rabbi, would have been married with a home and family to maintain. This distinction is very important in assessing the differences between the views expressed in the Old and New Testaments. The idea of a celibate, community life was very foreign in pre-Christian days where God's commandment to *"populate the earth abundantly and multiply in it"* (**Gen. 9:7**) was taken very seriously. It still is by orthodox Jews. There were exceptions—the inner circles of the Essenes who lived in Judea and a group called the Therapeutae who lived outside Alexandria in Egypt—but both were considered very unusual.

In early Biblical times, society depended mostly upon trade between individuals. Money, as we would understand it, was rare. It was first used *at all* approximately 500 years before the birth of Jesus. In much of the Hebrew Testament times, no coins were used and people bartered goods instead. The aristocracies and royal courts used jewels and precious metals as a form of currency but everyday people dealt with a more practical form of exchange such as swapping one produce for another.

As societies became more and more influenced by Greek and, later, Roman civilization, this like-for-like barter was replaced by weights of precious metals and then by coins. Generally in the Hebrew Testament, when an amount of silver or gold is given, such as ten shekels of silver, this refers to the actual weight of silver not ten silver coins. Pre-weighed metal coins, which were given the same names as the weight units, became a more convenient means of exchange as soon as travel became more commonplace and easier with the expansion of the Roman Empire.

Therefore, a great deal of the riches mentioned to in the Old Testament referred to a more general prosperity than a financial one. Signs of God's favor were seen in happiness and health as well as in business dealings. People as far back as Abraham and Sarah's times were just as frequently nomadic cattle-keepers as they were tillers of the ground so they would not necessarily have houses full of possessions in the way we do. In a nomadic, rural society, your wealth was pretty much everything you could carry or herd.

However, in **Genesis 13:2**, Abraham is described as being *"very rich in livestock and in silver and in gold"* so he is being portrayed as a aristocrat among men in a society where precious metals were deemed as valuable as they are today and were often worn in jewelry as an outer sign of wealth.

Jesus and money

With the Roman conquest of Judea, money became much more common and was associated with the hated invaders. Only Rome minted gold or silver coins of value; their colonies could only mint low values in bronze or copper. The Roman coins also had religious symbols and images on them which were anathema to the Jews. The people who collaborated and traded with the occupying force would also have been loathed and despised, as has been the case in every century since. Therefore it is entirely possible that Jesus and his followers might have looked upon Roman cash with a jaundiced eye.

However, this view does sit at odds with Jesus' association with tax collectors. These people (as is often still the case!) were disliked by their fellow men, especially the Pharisees and the scribes. Tax collectors to them were *"especially wicked sinners"* (**Matt. 9:10-11; Luke 15:1-3; Mark 2:15**). Reputedly, the collectors were allowed to gather more than the government asked and keep the excess amount. Some of these tax collectors were Roman but others were Jews.

Jesus set a startling new precedent by mingling with the Jewish tax collectors. He ate with them (**Mark 2:16**), showed them mercy and compassion (**Luke 19:9**), and he even chose a tax collector—Matthew—as one of his disciples (**Matt. 9:9**). Jesus even compared their willingness to repent of their sins with the arrogance of the Pharisees and scribes (**Luke 18:9-14; Matt. 9:11-13**).

Jesus is customarily assumed to have been poor (although this view is examined in Chapter Eight). Popular opinion certainly sees him as a poor, itinerant preacher despite the fact that, in the Gospel of Matthew, it's stated that the Magi brought him incredible wealth in the form of gold, frankincense and myrrh which were three of the most valuable commodities of the time.

He was also fond of eating and drinking with his friends. *"The son of man is come eating and drinking; and ye say, Behold a gluttonous man, and a winebibber, a friend of publicans and sinners!"* (**Luke 7:34**) so, although it would appear that early Christianity embraced the ideas of poverty, chastity and martyrdom with fervor, Jesus himself appeared to like having fun and good food. His very first miracle was turning water into wine so that there would be enough to make everything merry at the Marriage at Cana (**John 2:1-11**).

Much of the poverty consciousness that developed within Christianity may have been due to St. Paul's teachings and his acceptance of all-comers to the new faith. Paul indicated strongly that he believed that Jesus would return very soon and that both belief in him as Lord and a life of great virtue were required in advance of the Day of Judgment. There would be no point in amassing riches as the End of Days was coming within your lifetime.

In **1 Thessalonians 5:2-11**, Paul wrote:

"For yourselves know perfectly that the day of the Lord so cometh as a thief in the night. For when they shall say, Peace and safety; then sudden destruction cometh upon them, as travail upon a

woman with child; and they shall not escape. But ye, brethren, are not in darkness, that that day should overtake you as a thief. Ye are all the children of light, and the children of the day: we are not of the night, nor of darkness. Therefore let us not sleep, as do others; but let us watch and be sober."

The stories of saints and holy people within Christianity have always emphasized that they walked away from both marriage and money; that martyrdom was seen as holy and self-denial sacred. This is still evident in allegations that Blessed Mother Theresa of Calcutta believed that suffering would bring people closer to Jesus. *The Lancet* and *The British Medical Journal* have both criticized Mother Theresa and her staff for their failure to give painkillers to the sick. Sanal Edamaruki writing for *Rationalist International* claimed that in Mother Theresa's homes for the dying, you could *"hear the screams of people having maggots tweezered from their open wounds without pain relief"* adding that Mother Theresa's philosophy was that it was *"the most beautiful gift for a person that he can participate in the sufferings of Christ."*

Throughout the ages, we see differing views on worth or prosperity in interpretation of the Bible's teachings. Jesus and those who followed him lived at a time of great revolution in social affairs—a change as great as the invention of flight in the late 19th century. However, it is evident that Jesus did not automatically judge those who were wealthy—or even those who were thought to be misusing wealth by the general populace.

Chapter Five

The Torah and Tithing

The stories in the first five books of the Bible cover the creation, Adam and Eve, Noah's Ark, Abraham and Sarah, Isaac, Jacob, Joseph, the Exodus from Egypt and the journey to the Promised Land. The Torah also includes the laws followed by the Jewish faith and teachings repeated and elaborated on by Jesus including **Deuteronomy 6:5:**

> *"Thou shalt love the LORD thy God with all thine heart, and with all thy soul, and with all thy might."* Jesus expanded this to *"Thou shalt love the Lord thy God with all thy heart, and with all thy soul, and with all thy mind. This is the first and great commandment. And the second is like unto it, Thou shalt love thy neighbor as thyself. On these two commandments hang all the law and the prophets,"* (**Matt. 22:37**).

The prosperity teachings in the first five books of the Bible are both literal and metaphorical. Mystics interpret the Bible on four levels: literal, allegorical, personal and metaphysical, meaning the history, the moral, how the story relates to your own life and how it contributes to God's plan for humanity.

The story of the Exodus from Egypt, for example, is seen as a prosperity story about the escape from the slavery of convention and the rules of society to follow your own soul's path. The Israelites take a leap of faith in stepping out into the wilderness (which represents independence). The story makes it clear that there are plenty of trials and tests along the way and, even when you reach the Promised Land of the soul, there is still more psychological and spiritual work to be done. However, the

Hebrews were provided with *manna* all the way so that they could survive. *Manna* is usually translated as "the bread of heaven" but the Hebrew word *man* simply means "what is it?" So the lesson is that if we follow our spiritual path, we will be provided for but we won't necessarily understand how that will happen.

Anyone who has been divorced, left a safe job to go freelance or moved countries will be able to attest to the problems and delights of such an incredible journey.

Tithing

Probably the most used, and most freely interpreted, prosperity teachings of the Torah are the laws of tithing.

Many people think that tithing is a Biblical command to give the first ten per cent of your income to charity. Others believe that it is obligatory to give it to your church or synagogue. We'll look at all the details later but the first aspect to examine is the order of tithing. There are three tithes in the Old Testament: the first to God, the second for festivity and the third for charity.

It's the second tithe which is most frequently missed out in modern teaching but it is given quite as much attention in the Torah as the other two.

A tithe is traditionally ten per cent of someone's *increase*. That means any profit. Some modern churches recommend (or even insist) that their congregation tithe gross, to the church itself. However, back in Biblical times before money was widespread, the tenth would almost certainly have been produce or animals. If you didn't have ten more sheep than last year, you didn't have a tenth to tithe. If you grew olives, you would give a basket of olives; if you had chickens you would give a chicken or perhaps some eggs.

There is confusion about whether the tithes were voluntary or obligatory and whether they were considered to be required by God; an agreement with God or an unconditional gift to God. In the end, it's up to you as the teaching in Exodus, Leviticus, Deuteronomy and Numbers is so contradictory that it's impossible to say "this is exactly the way it should be." At the end of this chapter I will give you my own interpretation of how the tithes can be incredible prosperity teachings but the final decision is up to you.

Biblical Tithes

The first tithe we hear about is in the story of Cain and Abel in **Genesis 4:3**. Both men make an offering to God. Abel's was praised but Cain's was "not regarded." This is generally seen as meaning that God didn't like it but it may also be that God simply didn't see it (the Hebrew word *sha'ah* is translated by Strong's Hebrew dictionary as "look at, regard, gaze at or about").

The second tithe is from Abram and Sarai (before their names were changed to Abraham and Sarah) to Melchizedek, King of Salem who is described as a *"priest of the most high God."* Melchizedek had blessed Abraham and *"brought forth bread and wine"* (**Gen. 14:20**). This is the first indication of the covenant that would later become the Jewish Sabbath Eve ceremony and, later still, be transformed into the Last Supper and Christian Communion. This tithe sets a precedent of giving to a priest rather than directly to God in the form of a sacrifice. The priests worked at the Temple which was built after the Israelites made the Exodus from Egypt to the Promised Land. At that time, the first offering was given to the Levites, the descendents of Jacob's third son, Levi, who were in charge of the temple and all its activities. So it was a gift to those who maintained the place that brought inspiration or direct contact with God.

The third mention of tithing comes when Jacob, Abraham's grandson, has a dream where God promises to take care of him and his descendents.

"Then Jacob made a vow, saying, 'If God will be with me, and keep me in this way that I am going, and give me bread to eat and clothing to put on, so that I come back to my father's house in peace, then the LORD shall be my God. And this stone which I have set as a pillar shall be God's house, and of all that You give me I will surely give a tenth to You.'" (**Gen. 28:20**).

Some ministers dislike this story as it appears that Jacob is making a deal with God and they say that tithing is meant to be unconditional. But the Bible's characters are nothing if not human!

Tithing is then laid out in the three books of the Law given to Moses. Again, it is complicated but in a nutshell we are told of:

1. Tithe to the Lord. Annual. (**Lev. 27:30, Numbers 18:21-28**).
2. Festival Tithe. Annual. (**Deut. 12:6, 17-18; 14:22-27**).
3. Charity Tithe. Once every three years. (**Deut. 14:28; 26:12**).

Tithe number two, the Festival Tithe, was a second ten percent of one's increase set aside in order to feast in a place directed by God (most likely Jerusalem in later Biblical times though it doesn't specify). It indicates that we should celebrate with our families and, if we can't leave home, we are to organize a party with whatever meat and drink we fancy.

This appears to be a clear indicator that we are intended to rejoice in our lives and the gift of prosperity. We are to fill our own cup and replenish ourselves before we can be of service to others. Perhaps this is the meaning behind the phrase from the 23rd Psalm, *"My cup runneth over."* The Hebrew word used there is *revayah* meaning "saturated, running over or wealthy."

It may seem strange that the Charity Tithe was given only every third year but the Hebrews had a custom of leaving what was known as "gleanings" of every cut field or picked tree for the poor or homeless people to take to feed themselves. Also, family culture was very strong in Biblical times so most people would be taken care of in some way unless they preferred not to receive such charity or if they were deemed ritually unclean (such as a leper). However, the message is clear that although the care of others is important, it is not the first priority. It could be taken to mean that if we *all* learn to follow our true path and take care of ourselves, and teach others how to do the same, the need for giving would be lessened. Otherwise, we are giving from an empty vessel.

How tithing can be used in today's more secular world

In the modern world, Jews do not tithe. This is because the original tithe was for the Levites at the Temple and there is, now, no Temple. Instead, synagogues charge an annual fee for membership and upkeep. Any other gifts from their congregations are voluntary. However, Prosperity Gospel, Pentecostal and other evangelical churches and New Thought Churches encourage tithing—and even sometimes insist on it. So we can see, again, the confusion about whether this is meant to be a gift or a requirement.

Here is a modern interpretation of the system that I have used successfully in my prosperity teaching work for more than 20 years. Practicing it myself got me out of £50,000-worth of debt and brought me a life of great contentment. However, it is up to you to see if it works for you.

For those who have a spiritual rather than a religious belief, tithing may be interpreted in a slightly different way for the modern world. Give first towards spiritual inspiration, whether this is to your church, teacher or priest *or* money towards a retreat, a workshop or even a book that inspires you. Then give second for celebration/gifts for yourself and third to everybody else. The third tithe includes all payments to others including paying the bills (Biblical people didn't have telephone, gas, electricity, property tax, etc. so there was no injunction about those).

For those who have followed New Thought, New Age or Law of Attraction principles, this demonstrates to Spirit what your priorities are. You want firstly to be inspired (with ideas and creative opportunities to follow your life's path), secondly, you understand your value and seek fun and festivity and, thirdly, you wish to be prosperous enough to pay your dues and help others.

If you give to others first, you are telling God or the Universe that you do not value Spirit or yourself. Changing just this one aspect in their lives has helped countless people live more abundantly.

I do also recommend that people don't worry about the "tenth" aspect. In a world where wages often seem to be eaten up with everyday living costs, it is hard to know what the increase is. So the best way to try the practice out is to set aside any amount that you are comfortable with *first* before paying bills or giving to charity. This is the nearest equivalent to the Biblical teaching of the "first fruits" (**Proverbs 1:3**) and, if you are broke, it can simply mean one dollar, one pound or one euro.

If you are dealing with cash, you could have a couple of attractive bags or boxes, one for the inspiration tithe and one for the festival tithe. Place a coin or a note in the boxes when you receive it—before paying the bills. That money can then be saved up to buy something special or used immediately if appropriate. The important thing is that you have stated to yourself and to God that you seek inspiration and prosperity rather than debt or fear. It doesn't matter that you've saved $2 and then paid £500 in bills, you've still set your intention.

If your money goes directly into your bank, then you can have a couple of online savings accounts named, perhaps, "inspiration" and "celebration" and move £1/$1 (or more) into those accounts as soon as possible once money has come in. Only then pay the bills.

Although the Bible talks about the first ten per cent being

given to the Levites, this was because they spent their whole time caring for the Temple and looking after the people's religious needs. Nowadays, most conventional ministers are paid wages— and your priest may or may not be your source of inspiration. That is the key—what inspires you? What takes you closer to your own personal relationship with Divinity? Is it a book you'd like to buy? Is it a workshop you'd like to go to? Is it an inspirational teacher you'd like to hear? That's where to put your money. It may take you a few weeks to save up for what you want but the money is there, in the box or the savings account, putting a value on your spiritual growth and your right to enjoy God's abundance.

Of course it's fine to use your spiritual tithe as an unconditional gift for others who inspire you but be sure that you distinguish between giving from true inspiration and giving to support or help someone. That's the third tithe, not the first one.

There is also a fourth tithe in the Old Testament—the Sabbatical tithe (**Ex. 23:10-11; Deut. 15:1**). Every seventh year the land was rested and all debts forgiven. The land lay fallow so that it could replenish itself.

No Hebrew took on a debt for more than seven years—and, although they were expected to make every effort to repay it, if they could not then the amount was forgiven and forgotten as part of the seventh year.

Nowadays, some of the more prosperous countries are forgiving Third World Debt. That can only be a good thing—and what a wonderful world it would be if we all could forgive our debtors and have our own debts forgiven too.

Chapter Six

Prosperity Teachings in
The Ten Commandments

Until the Hebrew and New Testaments and the Talmud—the commentary on the Torah—were finally decided on and written down, the stories and teachings in the Bible were constantly debated in the Oral Tradition. Of course, people still do debate them but it's a challenge to balance ancient laws with mortgages, refrigerators, disinfectant, pets, lifestyles, humanitarian issues and over-population. To the orthodox Jew, the 613 Jewish laws of the Torah are inviolable and given by God. To the more liberal Jew and to the Christian, they were the form that was required at the time. Some of the 603 extra laws are still considered valid today and some are not; very few of us nowadays live in a society that would tolerate putting to death someone who worked on the Sabbath.

The Torah gives us the ten primary commandments three times; in **Exodus 20:2–17** and **34:1** and in **Deuteronomy 5:6-21**. The texts are virtually identical.

The first three commandments deal with our relationship with God. The other seven deal with our relationship with each other and the world. Some mystics call them the "ten advisements" rather than commandments.

The First Commandment

"I am the LORD thy God, which have brought thee out of the land of Egypt, out of the house of bondage. Thou shalt have no other gods before me."

It's worth noting that it doesn't say that there *are* no other gods; in Biblical days there were dozens of gods—Greek, Roman, Pagan, gods of the home, of work, of prosperity, of war, of love, of nature.

The gods of other nations were supposed to be anathema to the Israelites but archaeology has shown that figurines of gods and goddesses were found in Hebrew homes.

The modern esoteric meaning of this commandment however is wider: that if we do not put our own, individual relationship with Divinity first, then we cannot prosper. A god is not necessarily a mythical entity worshipped in a temple; it is anything that rules you to the extent that you do not question it. Nowadays, without realizing it, many regard fame, reputation, family, sex, football, money, work, drugs, social convention and television as gods. Putting these lesser gods before our relationship with the Holy One means that Grace cannot be received and life becomes either a repetitive cycle of fear or the search for highs that are followed by lows that ultimately lead to disillusionment.

Nowadays, for many, having a relationship with God does not necessarily mean going to church, mosque, temple or synagogue; it means dropping the pre-conceived, second-hand interpretations of Divinity that we learnt as children and making peace with the idea of a creative force for Good.

The second commandment is intended to help us to do just that.

The Second Commandment

"Thou shalt not make unto thee any graven image, or any likeness of any thing that is in heaven above, or that is in the earth beneath, or that is in the water under the earth. Thou shalt not bow down thyself to them, nor serve them: for I the Lord thy God am a jealous God, visiting the iniquity of the fathers upon the children unto the third and fourth [generation] *of them that hate me; And shewing*

mercy unto thousands of them that love me, and keep my commandments."

Judaism regards Christianity as essentially a Pagan religion because of its images of God. As the majority of Christians also believe that Christ is God, all the crucifixes in Church, around people's necks and on altars could also be seen as violations of this second commandment.

However, the commandment is not for no images at all but for no *graven* images. A graven image is set in stone, allowing no personal interpretation; no argument. The whole idea of the One God is that It is sexless, formless, absolute—not male, not female, not white nor black, not old nor young. The Hebrew for "the Lord God" in the Old Testament, *Yahweh Elohim*, is perhaps intended to reflect that. Hebrew has no neuter tense; *Yahweh* is masculine and *Elohim* has a feminine ending and can be both singular or plural according to the rest of the sentence.

Islam and orthodox Judaism take this commandment very seriously—there are few images of animals or humans in synagogues and none in mosques.

We live in a world of graven images. The "perfect" Western woman, for example, is a supermodel: size 6 or less, with smooth skin. Fewer than 2% of Western women actually look like that but nowadays there is Photoshop, Botox and surgery to ensure that the image is perpetuated.

Organic food was rejected for many years because "good" food is beautifully colored and has no worms, bugs or marks. Only once organic food looked as perfect as chemically-treated food did it find any kind of mass success.

This does not mean that we should not strive for excellence; just that we should guard against making one image the only right image.

The "jealous God" aspect of the second commandment also causes some problems in interpretation: it is generally thought to be a reference to the traditional judgmental Old Testament God.

In his book *Prosperity,* Charles Fillmore explains that the Hebrew word used for "jealous"—*kannaw*—means "jealous of principle." This principle, Charles explains, is the Universal Law—the law of karma; what you put out you get back. So this is an injunction that if we make our graven images and stand by them they are what we will receive in return. Interestingly, the word "generation" does not exist in the original Hebrew and has been added in later translation, apparently for clarity. It is possible that the sentence refers instead to our actions returning to us time and time again—"what goes around comes around" or the law of karma.

There is a great deal of resistance over the idea of reincarnation and karma in the Christian world although the Pharisaic belief in the possibility of multiple lives is referred to by the Jewish historian Josephus (*The Jewish War* 2.164): "the souls of good men only are removed into other bodies." The concept is also mentioned in the Gospels when the disciples tell Jesus that some people think he is Elijah come again or John the Baptist reborn. Also in the story of the blind man (**John 9:2**) where the disciples ask Jesus *"Who did sin, this man or his parents that he was born blind?"*

One of the reasons why the work of the early Church Father Origen was made anathema by the Nicean Council of 553 was due to his insistence on "the pre-existence of souls."

The Third Commandment

"Thou shalt not take the name of the Lord thy God in vain; for the Lord will not hold him guiltless that taketh his name in vain."

The Old Testament contains ten names for God. This commandment refers to the ultimate Name as given to Moses in **Exodus 3.13-15**.

"And Moses said unto God, Behold, when I come unto the children of Israel, and shall say unto them, The God of your fathers hath sent me unto you; and they shall say to me, What is his name? What shall I say unto them?

"And God said unto Moses, I AM THAT I AM: and he said, Thus shalt thou say unto the children of Israel, I AM hath sent me unto you."

God then adds:

"Thus shalt thou say unto the children of Israel, The Lord God of your fathers, the God of Abraham, the God of Isaac, and the God of Jacob, hath sent me unto you: this is my name for ever, and this is my memorial unto all generations."

This second name is *Yahweh Elohim* but, even so, the ultimate name is now believed by many simply to be Yahweh. Orthodox Jews do not even pronounce Yahweh out of respect. However, the primary name of God is *Eheyeh Asher Eheyeh.*

Biblical Hebrew doesn't have a present tense; it just has the perfect tense for a completed action and the imperfect tense for an incomplete action. Therefore scholars often translate *Eheyeh Asher Eheyeh* as "I Will Be That Which I Will Be."

However, "I" is used twice in whichever translation you prefer. For the mystic this refers to God the Transcendent: the Absolute All; and God the Immanent: the part within us that is also Divine. As children of God we are creative partners with God.

So to take the ultimate Name of God in vain may not be to blaspheme as in saying "oh my God!" but to misuse the phrases "I," "I Am" or "I Will Be."

To say "I am stupid; I am unworthy; I am no good" would be to take the ultimate name of God in vain — as is to make a promise such as "I promise to visit" and not doing it. Each one of us is a spark of Divinity incarnate; our every word is a command to the Universe so this commandment teaches us to use the Name wisely.

The Worldly Commandments

The fourth commandment *"Remember the Sabbath and keep it holy"* links the holy with everyday life. After this, all the commandments deal with living in the physical world. This one is an injunction to rest, relax and take one whole day off in a week to reconnect with ourselves and with God. In the modern world of 24-hour news, Internet, social networking and mobile phones, very few of us take a day away from the secular world to recoup. The Sabbath is intended to be a time of joy, not of boredom and, in a world of workaholism, is more than relevant today. When we don't take a day off, we close the door on being and allowing and therefore to our ability to receive prosperity.

The fifth commandment is *"Honor thy father and mother."* This, to the mystic, is an injunction to acknowledge the tradition of our birth even if we don't wish to embrace it. It does refer to our own parents, too, although it doesn't mean that we have to like them or even love them. If we understand where they come from and how they were raised, we can learn what poverty consciousness they taught on (though no fault of their own) so that we can amend ours.

"Do not murder." The sixth commandment is *not* do not kill; that is a misinterpretation dating back to St Jerome's translation of the Bible in the fourth century CE. Murder is a pre-meditated act and esoterically it includes destroying someone's emotional or spiritual life as well as physical life. It is murder to belittle someone's good idea or hopeful thoughts which are part of their essential prosperity consciousness. We do it to ourselves as well; destroying our spiritual goals by living in a way that is self-destructive or by thinking negative thoughts.

"Do not commit adultery." This means not mixing together two

things that harm each other. Marital infidelity is included but, in the esoteric view, it would be seen to be equally adulterous if two people who were damaging each other mentally and spiritually remained in such a destructive relationship.

"Do not steal." This includes theft of ideas or reputation or taking up so much of someone else's life by demanding attention that they have nothing left for themselves. It also refers to treating people as things or possessions rather than immortal souls.

"Thou shalt not bear false witness against thy neighbor." This is the giving of information that destroys good opinion—or which builds an inaccurate high opinion of someone or something. Marketing ploys are often false witness, as is gossip.

"Thou shalt not covet thy neighbor's house, thou shalt not covet thy neighbor's wife, nor his manservant, nor his maidservant, nor his ox, nor his ass, nor any thing that is thy neighbor's." This is advice to be grateful for what you have so that this can increase rather than wasting time in envy. Focusing on someone else's good fortune creates resentment which brings increasing feelings of lack and unhappiness. It doesn't mean that we can't admire what others have; rather that we should focus on creating our own prosperity instead of wasting energy destructively.

The 603 Commandments

The Hebrews followed a further 603 laws still observed, wherever possible, by orthodox Jews today. Of these laws (which are spread throughout Exodus, Numbers, Deuteronomy and Leviticus) quite a few still make good sense but they are all of their time.

Some of the 603 include:

- Not to demand from a poor man repayment of his debt, when the creditor knows that he cannot pay (**Ex. 22:24**).
- Not to delay payment of a hired man's wages (**Lev. 19:13**).

- Not to decide a court case on the evidence of a single witness (**Deut. 19:15**).
- Not to take a bribe (**Ex. 23:8**).

Some of the laws cannot be followed because they refer to a time when the Jewish Temple existed. Some are deemed unacceptable to all but the most died-in-the-wool orthodox Jew, fundamentalist Christian or anyone who supports the death penalty. These include the laws that everyone who does not believe in God, anyone who curses their father or mother and everyone who commits adultery should be put to death—and that anyone bleeding is unclean and defiles others if touched.

We can barely imagine the kind of lives that people lived in the time of the Exodus. In an environment lacking totally in insect-repellent, sanitation or sterilizing agents, every care had to be taken to avoid anything that could attract disease which could prove fatal to a tribe.

In the case of adultery or cursing your parents, you only have to watch a modern soap opera to know that even today there are those who would use such happenings to start a fight. In a world without hospitals, a fight could mean disfigurement, injury and death—and lead to further fights in revenge.

In the case of homosexuality, **Deuteronomy 23:17** states, *"There shall be no whore of the daughters of Israel, nor a sodomite of the sons of Israel."* The Hebrew words used for whore and sodomite are *quedeshaw* and *qadesh* which mean female or male temple prostitute. Worshippers at the temples of those gods would have sex with these prostitutes who represented the god itself. This would have been a complete abomination to the Israelites. In **Leviticus 18:22** which condemns intercourse between males, death is not the penalty and the law is given no more power than an earlier injunction not to have sex with both a mother and her daughter.

Of all these laws, the most important thing to remember is

that the Jewish nation continually debated interpretations of them—and still do. Nothing is set in stone; nothing is a graven image.

Chapter Seven

Kings and Prophets

The Hebrew Bible is divided into three sections: *Torah, Prophets* and *Writings*. The latter books are less well-known than the Torah but they contain many familiar names such as Samson, Saul, David, Solomon, Ruth and Esther.

Like the Torah, the Prophets and Writings have their fair share of massacres, smitings and tragedies but they also have some wonderful prosperity stories. There isn't room to list them all here so we will focus on three which demonstrate powerful laws of abundance.

What is interesting to note is a pattern throughout Torah and the other writings where the main characters leave their homes and travel to a new country. It seems that they all have to step out of the comfort of family and the everyday habits of life in order to find their good and serve the Holy One. Custom and habit often speak louder than the "still silent voice" of truth but it is our soul's call that will prosper us and the world.

Trusting That More Will Come

One of the hardest things to do when money or supplies run short is to keep trusting that more is coming. Again and again, the Bible tells us to have faith in God *"Thou shalt remember the Lord thy God for it is He that giveth you the power to get wealth"* (**Deut. 8:18**). To cut back, worry about our bills, go to a cheaper supermarket and cancel the holiday are not actions of someone with a prosperity consciousness. The Bible tells us that we simply *have* to trust or we will put more power into our negative thoughts than in God's will for us and what we fear will come to pass.

In the *Book of Kings*, the Lord tells the prophet Elijah to leave Israel. Elijah is told he will be fed by ravens by a brook which is similar to the manna from heaven provided for the Hebrews in the wilderness in the Exodus from Egypt. When the brook dries up, God sends Elijah to a widow in Phoenicia. Elijah asks the widow for some food and she replies that she only has flour and oil and not enough of those to feed her and her son, let alone a stranger. Elijah says to her, *"Fear not ... For thus saith the Lord God of Israel, The barrel of meal shall not waste, neither shall the cruse of oil fail, until the day that the Lord sendeth rain upon the earth"* (**1 Kings 17:14**).

The widow believes him, feeds him with the last of their food and Elijah's prophesy miraculously comes true; thus, by an act of faith the woman receives the promised blessing. Interestingly, she is not an Israelite but a foreigner. Again and again, throughout the Bible, it is shown that more faith is demonstrated by people who are away from the Hebrew tribal consciousness. Jesus says of the Roman Centurion who asks him to heal a much-loved servant, *"I say unto you, I have not found so great faith, no, not in Israel"* (**Luke 7:9**).

Digging Your Ditches

Similar conviction is shown by the prophet Elisha. Instead of jumping into action when faced with a problem, he takes some time out to listen to God's word.

Jehoram, the king of Israel, and Jehoshaphat, the king of Judah, together were marching to war against Moab. They had enough livestock with them to feed three armies and had been marching for seven days when they ran out of water.

Jehoram blamed God for their predicament but Jehoshaphat went for advice to the prophet Elisha who simply said, *"now bring me a minstrel"* **2 Kings 3:15**.

Here is the principle of the Sabbath—stepping back, relaxing in order to allow the word of God to come instead of rushing into what we "ought" to do.

To powerful kings representing three nations and their armies, the prophet said, *"Call me a minstrel. And it came about, when the minstrel played, that the hand of the Lord came upon him. And he said, 'Make this valley full of ditches.'"*

There was no sign of rain but Elisha was certain that they had to demonstrate that they were expecting their good. They were to dig ditches in the desert where there was no water and where there was no indication that there would be water.

The solution to their problem was to be obedient to the word of the Lord—regardless of what the circumstances were. The prosperity teaching is that trust and preparation for our blessings is absolutely essential. If we want to get an interview for a new job and we need a haircut, get the haircut before we hear about the interview. It's taking the step of faith instead of giving power to our doubts.

Once the ditches were dug, floods of water filled them to the brim (**2 Kings 3:20**).

Coming Into The Kingdom

There are only two books in the Bible which have women's names as their titles: *Ruth* and *Esther*. Both tell of women who leave their tribe. Ruth the Moabite follows her Hebrew mother-in-law whose beliefs she has come to love and trust, speaking one of the most beautiful passages in the Bible:

> *"Entreat me not to leave thee, to return from following after thee: for whither thou goest, I will go; and where thou lodgest, I will lodge: thy people shall be my people, and thy God my God"* (**Ruth 1:16**).

Ruth later marries a wealthy Hebrew, Boaz, and, even though she is not Jewish, she becomes the ancestor of King David and also of Jesus. So even though orthodox Judaism insists that Jew marries Jew, the Hebrew Bible tells the faithful to step out of the tribe when required because a true believer in God is of more worth than a tribal custom.

The Jewish festival of Purim is based around *The Book of Esther* and the prosperity message of the story is about stepping up to become our true selves.

Esther is a Jewess living in exile in Persia. The king, Ahasuerus, has divorced his first wife and is seeking a new one. He is so powerful that he doesn't need to marry a foreign princess so all the loveliest women in his kingdom take part in a beauty contest in their province to be selected. All the winners get to spend an evening with the king and he will choose his queen from among them.

Esther is persuaded to take part by her uncle, Mordecai. This is despite the fact that Judaism forbids intermarriage. Like Cinderella she wins through, charms her prince and becomes queen of Persia.

However, this story does not end with "they got married and lived happily ever after." Mordecai has persuaded Esther not to tell Ahasuerus that she is a Jew so she begins her reign without her husband knowing who she truly is. When a crisis looms and Ahasuerus's wicked favorite, Haman, plans a massacre of the Jews, Mordecai asks Esther to intervene but she tells him she can't. She hasn't seen her husband in private in 30 days which, for a new bride with no children yet, indicates a big problem. Even worse, anyone who went to the King of Persia without his express permission was killed, unless he extended mercy.

Mordecai sends Esther a message saying, *"If thou altogether holdest thy peace at this time, then shall there enlargement and deliverance arise to the Jews from another place; but thou and thy father's house shall be destroyed: and who knoweth whether thou art come into the kingdom for such a time as this?"* (**Esther 4:11**).

Some Bible translations use "royalty" but the Hebrew word is *Malkhuth* which means "kingdom". Jesus, of course, speaks of the kingdom of heaven and the kingdom of God in the New Testament.

Esther then tells Mordecai to get the Jewish people to pray and to fast for her for three days and promises that she will go in to the king even though she realizes that she may die. Her husband has already disposed of one unpopular wife.

On the third day, Esther puts on her "kingdom" (usually translated as "royal apparel") and goes before the king. She realizes that she is the Queen of Persia and she needs to start acting like it even if she is going to have to give her life for her people.

The king is delighted. He grants his wife mercy and asks her what she wants, saying that it will be given to her, up to the value of half his kingdom. So it is quite likely that it was Esther who had withdrawn from him, through feeling unworthy.

Then Esther is very clever—and again uses the Sabbath principle of waiting and taking time out. She invites the king and Haman to a banquet in her apartments on two successive nights. She does not ask that the king spare the Jews; instead making it clear that she wants her husband's company. Some mystics interpret this as Esther (the human soul) demonstrating that she desires the King's (God's) love before all other things (the first tithe).

Then, when the king asks Esther at the end of the second evening what he can do for her in return, she asks simply for him to save her own life and the life of her people. When Ahasuerus asks who has condemned them, she indicates Haman, giving the king a clear choice between his servant and his wife. She does not coerce; she does not push. She trusts in God, stands in the kingdom and waits for her husband's decision.

Her petition is granted and the Jews saved.

Esther's story is important because, like Elisha's, it focuses on taking time for God and for self before taking action. In Esther's case this is not listening to music but honoring her true inner royalty. She would have put on her robes and her crown—celebration robes—to go before the king and this also honored God's work in making her Queen of Persia and the potential savior of her people. This takes us again to the three laws of tithing—God, self, others—and to the 23rd Psalm: "*My cup runneth over.*" We have to fill ourselves with God's glory and with rest and with peace and joy before we can do good work in the world. Otherwise we are running on empty and setting a poor example to those who are seeking our help.

Chapter Eight

Was Jesus poor?

Many theologians and priests believe that Jesus of Nazareth was poor despite the fact that there is little evidence of such poverty in the New Testament. He was certainly a travelling preacher who lived with few possessions but, in the Biblical world where many were nomads or cattle herders, this was not necessarily an indication of poverty. Such people were welcomed in settlements where there was an ancient Hebrew custom of leaving food out for holy men and women as one of life's duties.

What we take to be evidence of lack could be simply a misinterpretation of an ancient lifestyle. Certainly, Jesus was not a fan of cluttering yourself up with possessions so that you were too tied down by responsibilities to be able to follow your heart and soul. But it is quite possible to view his life as a series of miracles of prosperity beginning with his birth and continuing through to his death and resurrection.

Jesus is held up as a paragon of virtue due to his life as an itinerant preacher with no possessions. This belief in self-denial has been adhered to—and added to—by Christians for centuries. Most saints from ancient times lived lives of self-sacrifice and self-mortification, offering us horrific examples of what it means to be holy. St. Francis and St. Clare lived lives of such self-denial that they became physically ill. We are told of virgins who mutilated themselves to avoid being found attractive or forced to marry; and at the very least of men and women who threw off their robes of wealth, dressed in coarse cloth and shut themselves away from all society to devote their lives to prayer. St. Rose of Lima, from the age of 20, wore a metal spiked crown, concealed by roses, and an iron chain about her waist. She would fast for days, taking just a drink of bitter herbs and when she could no longer stand, she sought repose on a bed, constructed by herself, of broken glass, stone, potsherds and thorns. In today's world, Rose would be considered mentally ill, anorexic or deluded.

Carpenter or Stonemason?

We are taught that Jesus was a carpenter but even this is disputed. **Mark 6:3** has the people in the synagogue in Nazareth saying, *"Is not this the carpenter…?"* But in the parallel story in **Matthew 13: 55** Jesus is referred to only as the carpenter's son and not as a carpenter himself.

Either way, the implication is that this was not an impressive thing to be. But the Greek word translated as "carpenter" in the Gospels is *tekton* which actually meant artisan, mason or builder rather than just "a worker in wood."

Richard A. Batey, in his *Jesus & the Forgotten City: New Light on Sepphoris and the Urban World of Jesus* (Baker 1992) defines *tekton* as "a skilled worker who works on some hard material such as wood or stone or even horn or ivory … the tasks performed by carpenters and masons could easily overlap."

The Talmud is often quoted as using the fact that Jesus was a carpenter as an insult but, putting aside attributed references to someone whom the ancient Jews saw simultaneously as an impostor and a threat, the trade of carpenter itself is shown as being deeply respected. According to the scholar Yacob Levy there is a Talmudic story of a man who arrives in a town looking for someone to help him with a religious problem. He asks for the rabbi but, when he finds that there is no rabbi there, he says, *"Is there a carpenter among you, the son of a carpenter, who can offer me a solution?"* (*Wörterbuch über Talmudim und Midrachim*, Berlin 1924). This appears to indicate that where there was no rabbi, a carpenter was the person most qualified to interpret law or answer questions.

It is one thing to have a trade and another to have customers. Wood-workers built tools for farmers such as ploughs, yokes, winnowing forks and threshing sledges and stonemasons built houses but, in a settlement like Nazareth, there might not be that much call for such work. However, four miles from Jesus' home town there was a property boom offering enough employment for a dozen *tektons*.

The town of Sepphoris was the capital city of Herod the Great's son, Herod Antipas, the client-king of Judea ("client" because he was subject to Rome and ruled under the Emperor). It had been partially destroyed by fire in about 4 BCE and during Jesus' youth was being rebuilt into a modern, thriving city. Like most of the other wealthy Jewish cities in the Roman period, it leant towards Greco-Roman architecture and design. Archaeologists are still discovering luxurious homes and public buildings dating back to the first century; there was an aqueduct and a palace and there is still controversy among archaeologists as to whether the great theatre of Sepphoris was completed before or after Jesus' lifetime.

As glass was one of the main industries of the area, the very least that would have been needed of a carpenter who only worked with wood would have been doors and windowsills in their thousands. For a man with a wider range of talents, the work would be full-time for years on end. The four-mile walk from Nazareth would be considered a very reasonable commute and the pay more than adequate.

Was Jesus despised?

When putting forward any hypothesis, it's important to acknowledge the oppositions to it and the best example of a popular work where Jesus is emphatically deemed to be poor, despised and rejected and simultaneously someone who would never deign to work in Sepphoris is Bruce Chilton's book *Rabbi Jesus* (Image).

Chilton surmises that Jesus was a *mamzer*, the Hebrew word for outcast. This equates to the Hindu caste of untouchables. His logic is that Jesus was illegitimate and of unknown parentage which led to his never being allowed in synagogue, probably running away from home at the age of 12 and living rough for most of his life. But Chilton also says that Jesus would not have been willing to work in Sepphoris, which was Herod Antipas's town, as he would have viewed it as unclean. Sepphoris is known to have been the site of a *yeshiva* or school of religious study and oral tradition in the first century CE. (*Jerusalem Talmud*) and there is ample evidence that the most humble through to the ultra-orthodox did visit there.

Whatever your belief in Jesus' conception, whether it was human or Divine, both the Gospels of Matthew and Luke make it clear that his earthly father Joseph acknowledged and accepted him. If Jesus were an outcast, he would not be allowed in the synagogue or temple and could never be called *Rabbi*. According to the Gospels, Jesus attains all those things. For all those reasons, it's fair to dispute the *mamzer* theory strongly. It is also worth noting that, in Jesus' day, the title of Rabbi was only given to men who were either married or widowed. For further debate on that matter, see my book *The Marriage of Jesus* (O Books). So, it is probably fair to begin with the child of an artisan who was probably doing fairly well—and might even have been considered the equivalent of Middle Class (and therefore possibly despised by both working class and aristocrat!)

Birth in the Stable

Jesus' birth in a stable is also used as evidence of a poverty-stricken start in life and we need to look at this legend in detail not only for the levels of interpretation of this story itself but as an indication of how hard it is to ensure that clear translations have been used of the original New Testament Greek in any other aspects of Jesus' life and teachings.

The nativity story of Jesus as we see it portrayed in books and films is that Joseph and Mary went from Nazareth to Bethlehem to be taxed with Mary heavily pregnant riding a donkey. They tried every lodging house in Bethlehem but were unable to find a single inn that could offer them accommodation and eventually had to sleep in a stable with the ox and the donkey where Mary gave birth.

This story is in the *Gospel of Luke* and it reads:

"And Joseph also went up from Galilee, out of the city of Nazareth, into Judaea, unto the city of David, which is called Bethlehem; (because he was of the house and lineage of David) to be taxed with Mary his espoused wife, being great with child.

"And so it was, that, while they were there, the days were accomplished that she should be delivered. And she brought forth her firstborn son, and wrapped him in swaddling clothes, and laid him in a manger; because there was no room for them in the inn" (**Luke 2:4-7**).

There is no donkey; no ox; no trailing around Bethlehem, no unkind inn-keepers and not even the slightest hint that Mary was in labor while they searched for somewhere to stay. *The Infancy Gospel of James,* one of the Nag Hammadi library scrolls, does say that Mary came into labor before they reached their destination and Joseph had to find somewhere in the countryside and a midwife. But there is no rejection; just details of simple practicalities.

Even so, the common assumption is made that Mary had to be in a stable because all the rooms in the inns were full. A lodging house in Jesus' day was made up from two dormitories with men and women segregated from each other. This meant that more people could stay at a time of pilgrimage and made it easier with respect to the laws of purity (where orthodox Jewish couples spent up to two weeks apart during and after the woman's menses). No woman giving birth would have been welcome in a dormitory room because she would have rendered all the others unclean.

It is also worth noting that a stable was not always separate from a house; animals were frequently kept just the other side of a barrier within the building itself; their body warmth being useful for the family and also to keep the beasts safe from theft.

So here we have the young Mary, about to give birth to her first child, in a warm place, where no one has to be worried about the ritual purity laws and the blood and natural mess of a baby's birth giving anyone else a problem.

Jewish Custom

Luke writes that Joseph was of the House of David and had to return to his family's hometown for the census (*apographo*, meaning "written record" rather than the usually-translated "tax") so, given the natural family ties within the Jewish nation, it's more than likely that he had some sort of extended family in the town.

It has been suggested before by scholars that Joseph and Mary would have stayed with relatives rather than at an inn (C. S. Keener, *Bible Background Commentary*, 194; B. Witherington, *Birth of Jesus*, DJG, 69-70), and common knowledge dictates that no Jewish family would allow even a distant cousin to stay in an inn if he could have stayed in the homes of their relatives. The word generally translated as "inn" is *kataluma* which more frequently means private guest room and is also used in **Luke 22:11** when Jesus sends his disciples to find a room to eat the Last Supper. The word for an inn with shared lodging is *pandocheion* (see the story of the Good Samaritan).

Even a private house may well have had a room where animals were kept and where straw was freely available to absorb fluids. And the stone (not wood) manger would have made an excellent and secure cradle when the baby was born.

The only reference to Jesus' birth in the other Gospels is in Matthew where the *magi* (astrologer priests) follow the star to find Mary and the child. They go first to Herod in Jerusalem and then directly to Bethlehem. There, they definitely visit an *oikia* (house) not a stable nor an inn. There's no evidence that Joseph and Mary have just moved to the town; rather Matthew thinks that they lived there already and only settled in Nazareth after their exile period in Egypt.

So, we have to conclude that we cannot possibly know whether or not Jesus was born into poverty. However, the Gospel evidence points towards its being unlikely.

Support for Spiritual Teachers

All the great spiritual teachers throughout time have had access to people who fund them and take care of them—so that they could focus on the work that they need to do without distractions. They were supported by other people's wealth; by people like us. This includes Jesus—**Luke 8:3** states clearly that he had financial support: *"Joanna the wife of Chuza Herod's steward, and Susanna, and many others, which ministered unto him of their substance (huparchonta*—wealth, possessions, or property).*"

It's worth noting that Ghandi's simple life came at a cost, as the poet Sarojini Naidu joked: *"If only Bapu knew the cost of setting him up in poverty!"* His philosophy taught village life in preference to that of the city, yet he was financially dependent on the support of industrial billionaires like the merchant prince, Ghanshyam Das Birla. Ghandi had an enormous entourage around him. Quite rightly; he needed it to be as effective as he was.

Buddha took "the middle path," of moderation between the extremes of sensual indulgence and self-mortification and Jesus did the same, leading a life of simple abundance without emphasis on possessions or attachment. That is one of the greatest secrets of prosperity—to allow it to flow to us and through us without needing to hold onto it or tie it down.

Chapter Nine

Jesus' teachings on prosperity

At first glance, Jesus' teachings appear to urge us to get rid of all possessions. However they also demonstrate that abundance falls like the rain from heaven if we just ask.

For many people, the idea of being without the latest technology, a good car, a comfortable home and money in the bank, is terrifying. But the majority of people in Galilee in Jesus' day didn't even have a dinner service for when friends went round for supper; guests expected to take their own bowl and spoon.

We live in a very different world but perhaps Jesus is not so much telling us to dispose of everything we own as to lose our attachment to it.

Buddha said that the origin of suffering is attachment. Attachment is similar to coveting, in that we may get obsessed with the idea that we "must" have an iPad or live in a certain school district so that our children can get the "right" education. But if nobody else wanted any of those things, most likely we wouldn't want them as much ourselves. Most marketing techniques are based on the theory of telling people that they are somehow lesser or unattractive if they don't use a certain product and that they will achieve status if they are among the first to purchase it.

Firstly though let's look at Jesus' teachings on how to manifest what you desire.

Perhaps the best-known is *"Ask and it shall be given you, seek and ye shall find; knock and it shall be opened unto you."* (**Matt. 7:7**) which is expanded to *"all things, whatsoever ye shall ask in prayer, believing, ye shall receive,"* later on in the same gospel (**Matt. 21:22**).

The same idea is the basis of the teachings in the best-selling DVD and book *The Secret* by Rhonda Byrne (Simon & Schuster) and many other modern prosperity teachings. I can state with hand on heart that it works—but the key is the believing part. Most of those with prosperity issues block their own abundance because they don't believe that they are worthy or that they should have what they want. And sometimes, too, you don't get what you asked for but you *do* get an equivalent good. You might not get the pay rise you want but you might get a rent reduction instead.

That Jesus, himself, could draw prosperity through belief is made clear in the only one of his miracles that is told in all four Gospels—the feeding of the five thousand with the loaves and the fishes (**Matt 14:13**, **Mark 6.31**, **Luke 9:10** and **John 6:5**).

His teaching is simple: you are worthy—believe. "*Consider the lilies of the field; how they grow. They toil not, neither do they spin. And yet, I say unto you, Solomon in all his glory was not arrayed like one of these.*" **Matt 6:28**. Somewhat at odds with the Protestant work ethic!

What is not always remembered is that Jesus was certain that we can do as much, or more, than he could.

"*I say unto you, He that believeth on me, the works that I do shall he do also; and greater than these shall he do,*" **John 14:12**. It's worth suggesting that you don't have to be a Christian to believe in the healing miracles of Jesus so that is a much less limiting statement than it may appear. It could be seen as just as much a statement of believing in the Christ consciousness within you whether or not you link it with the persona of Jesus.

The Eye of the Needle

Probably Jesus' best-known teaching around prosperity is "*It is easier for a camel to go through the eye of a needle, than for a rich man to enter into the kingdom of God.*" **Mark 10:25**.

Here's the story: A young man goes up to Jesus and asks him

what he should do to attain eternal life.

Jesus replies to keep the commandments.

The young man says he has always done so; what else does he lack? And Jesus answers:

> "'If thou wilt be perfect, go sell that thou hast, and give to the poor, and thou shalt have treasure in heaven: and come follow me.' But when the young man heard that saying, he went away sorrowful: for he had great possessions.
>
> "Then said Jesus unto his disciples, 'Verily I say unto you, That a rich man shall hardly enter into the kingdom of heaven.
>
> "And again I say unto you, it is easier for a camel to go through the eye of a needle, than for a rich man to enter into the kingdom of God.'"

There is a nice theory that "the Eye of the Needle" was the name of a narrow gate into Jerusalem and a camel could only pass through if its load of baggage was removed. Unfortunately there is no evidence for this.

The Aramaic word *gamla*, meaning "rope", is similar phonetically to the Greek *kamelos*. Jesus would have been speaking in his native Aramaic but his words were first written down in Greek, so this transliteration is possible. "Rope" makes more sense in the context of "needle."

However, this is actually not a saying that is unique to Jesus, E. W. Bullinger in his *Companion Bible* (Kregel Publications) writes that it is a proverb, common in the East. It is even in the Babylonian Talmud, although an elephant is substituted for a camel.

In the modern world, money and possessions frequently seem to be the be-all and end-all for many people. Jesus warns against this again in **Luke 12:15**: "*Take heed, and beware of covetousness: for a man's life consisteth not in the abundance of the things which he possesseth.*" The word for "covetousness" is *pleonexia*, best translated as "the greedy desire to have more." He also had strong feelings about what attachment to our possessions could do to us. *"What shall it profit a man, if he shall gain the whole world, and lose his own soul?"* **Mark 8:36**. And he warns against collecting treasure on earth where they can be stolen or corrupted. *"For where your treasure is, there shall your heart be also."* **Matt. 6:21**.

Again, there's no stipulation that we should never have possessions but that they may make it harder for us to follow a spiritually-led life if we are attached to them.

It's also clear that Jesus wasn't a fan of trade in holy places:

> *"And Jesus went into the temple of God, and cast out all them that sold and bought in the temple, and overthrew the tables of the moneychangers, and the seats of them that sold doves."* **Matt 21:12**—similar in **John 2:14**.

So there is a distinct theme emerging that there is a place for everything and everything in its place. The Temple is not the place for material transactions and as the Temple is the place of the Holy One we have to understand that there is a difference between our spiritual and material lives.

God and Mammon

Nearly everyone has heard Jesus' teaching, *"You cannot serve both God and mammon"* **Matt. 6:24**. But now we come to what is possibly Jesus' strangest teaching about money itself. The *mammon* quotation is also in the Gospel of Luke but, there, it follows a parable about a land steward which has perplexed theologians and scholars for centuries as it appears to contradict practically everything else that Jesus teaches on the subject. Here it is in full.

> *"There was a certain rich man, which had a steward; and the same was accused unto him that he had wasted his goods. And he called*

him, and said unto him, 'How is it that I hear this of thee? Give an account of thy stewardship; for thou mayest be no longer steward.' Then the steward said within himself, 'What shall I do? For my lord taketh away from me the stewardship: I cannot dig; to beg I am ashamed. I am resolved what to do, that, when I am put out of the stewardship, they may receive me into their houses.' So he called every one of his lord's debtors unto him, and said unto the first, 'How much owest thou unto my lord?' And he said, 'An hundred measures of oil.' And he said unto him, 'Take thy bill, and sit down quickly, and write fifty.' Then said he to another, 'And how much owest thou?' And he said, 'An hundred measures of wheat.' And he said unto him, 'Take thy bill, and write fourscore.' And the lord commended the unjust steward, because he had done wisely: for the children of this world are in their generation wiser than the children of light. And I say unto you, make to yourselves friends of the mammon of unrighteousness; that, when ye fail, they may receive you into everlasting habitations.

He that is faithful in that which is least is faithful also in much; and he that is unjust in the least is also unjust in much. If therefore, ye have not been faithful in that which is another man's who shall give you that which is your own? No servant can serve two masters for either he shall hate the one, and love the other, or else he will hold on to one and despise the other. Ye cannot serve God and mammon." (**Luke 16:1-13**).

There's a lot to take in here. At first glance it looks as though Jesus is commending dishonesty.

However, the first thing to do is have a look at the Greek. In the first line, the steward is accused of wasting the master's goods. The word used for "accused" is *diabolos* which more commonly means "slander" or "defame." So we don't actually know whether this steward—who would have been a land manager, collecting rents for the land owner—was incompetent, dishonest or just maligned.

Using your talents

It is generally thought to be fair to assume that, in Jesus' parables, "Master" refers to God. So it is possible that the steward is accused of wasting his talents or gifts. That takes us on a diversion to the parable of the talents (**Matt. 25: 15-28**) where a man going on a journey entrusts his money to his servants. The two servants entrusted with the most invest the money and give the man twice as much when he returns. But the third man buries the one talent he has and is derided for doing so.

It's fortunate for us that the Greek word *talanton* meaning "a weight of precious metal equal to a certain amount of money" translates as "talent" because it helps us with the parable. If God has given us gifts, he wants us to use and develop them to the full. But it would appear that if we have money, he also wants us to be creative with it.

How does this relate to the steward? He is told that he can no longer manage the Lord's affairs and he goes out to all the debtors and tells them to pay what they can, not what is literally calculated to be their debt. He is then praised by the master.

Given the common situation in Jesus' day of rent and tax collectors over-collecting from people, it could be that the steward was making reparation for previous over-payments. But this also works as a prosperity story if you can see the debtors as the "talents" or perhaps even the ego of the steward. He's been wasting his life but, when called to account by God, he does everything he reasonably knows he can do within the parameters of possibility to show his willingness to make amends.

So perhaps Jesus is saying that we have to do the best we can with the circumstances around us as well as making reparation for previous greed. "False mammon" is everywhere in the world with people being more concerned with finances and new gadgets than with other people or with God, so it is up to us to be at peace with that and live our best life anyway. It's certainly true that the "children of the world"—material people—are cannier than the "children of light" who can be very naïve in worldly matters. Maybe those of us who seek to be spiritual need to be practical too (after all, we too have to pay the rent).

But what is most clear is the idea that we should be comfortable with money and the good it can do but we should not make it our God (see the first commandment). That means not blaming it or hating it—or the people who have it—as well as not worshiping it.

This leads us neatly to another often perplexing quotation:

"For he that hath, to him shall be given; and he that hath not, from him shall be taken even that which he hath." **Mark 4:25**.

To a traditional thinker, that seems terribly unfair but to a New Thought teacher or a modern day follower of positive thinking this is clearly demonstrating that if we appreciate what we do have and focus on the good that is already in our lives, we will draw more good things to us. However, if we focus on the negative and how little we have, and how others have more than us, then we will become even more unhappy and therefore less prosperous. If you were God and had a gift to give, would you prefer to give it to someone who was appreciative of the good in their existing life or to someone who was grumpy, ungrateful and saw no good in anything?

It's fair to say that Jesus' teachings on money are complex and wide-ranging. But always, he returns to the principle that good and abundance is there for us every minute as long as we don't allow our possessions to possess us. If we don't "deny ourselves" (i.e. be willing to live without the stuff our ego desires to keep up with the Joneses), we can't allow the prosperity of each moment to flow. The best riches are here, now—not in a discarnate heaven, but in the natural abundance of God's grace in our lives.

It's not an easy lesson, especially in the commodities-ruled Western World. But it is a very powerful one.

Chapter Ten

Money and St. Paul

After the crucifixion, Jesus' message was spread by word of mouth by his disciples and others. Although Simon Peter overcame the Jewish law concerning unclean foods after a vision from God (**Acts 10:9**), and the apostles accepted uncircumcised converts (**Acts 15:7**), the teaching was still based on the roots of Judaism and the laws of the Torah. It was disseminated either locally or through the network of Jewish groups around the Mediterranean but it was rigorously opposed, not least by Saul of Tarsus until his conversion on the road to Damascus. Then, as Paul, he was to become its greatest proponent.

These were tempestuous years as the Jewish people were in revolt against the controlling Roman Empire, which was to lead to the destruction of the Temple in Jerusalem in 70CE. This was a body-blow to both the religious and political heart of the Jewish nation and spurred the Jewish scholars into writing down the sacred oral teaching in the form of Talmud, the commentary on Torah. The messianic Jews of Jerusalem began writing the Gospels at approximately the same time; not so much because of the fall of the Temple but to open the teaching up to a much wider range of people.

St Paul's letters pre-date any of the written Gospels. Without knowing it, he was shaping a new religion for centuries to come. Paul committed his view of the teaching to parchment and, in lieu of anything else from Jerusalem, these letters were copied by scribes and spread throughout the Roman Empire. Paul's writings were practical, sensible and wide-ranging, offering guidance for both gentiles and Jews alike. They are also very human.

The life and times of Paul

Paul is often unjustly criticized as we don't understand the pressures and social conventions that he was facing. For example, his injunction to women to cover their heads and not to prophesy in the streets was given at a time when the cult of Cybele or Magna Mater was at its height in Rome. This goddess's priests, the *galli*, were self-castrated men who wore women's clothes, long hair and shaved their bodies. They were viewed with horror—and often attacked—during their parades. At their major festival in March they mourned the death of the goddess's son Attis and then danced with joy at his resurrection on the third day. A Christian woman could be abused, insulted or even killed if she were to be mistaken for a priest of Cybele.

Added to that, Paul was a Jew and Jewish women *did* cover their heads and stay silent in synagogue; they still do in orthodox Jewry. That he raised the issue at all meant that Christian women were going bare-headed and preaching; you don't have to speak out against something if nobody is doing it.

Paul's letters are just that—letters. Much of the content is irrelevant to us and it is even possible that Paul would be horrified to know that a few somewhat irritated business letters he wrote to colleagues who were misbehaving were regarded as gospel 2,000 years on.

Paul wrote with strong emotion. He does not hesitate to call his followers "stupid" (**Gal. 3:1**) and he is more than firm on opposing Pagan infiltration into the groups setting up as Christians. However, he understands the nature of the people to whom he is writing. His Jewish background filters into the teaching and confirms the basics of the ten commandments. But he sets people free from the 603 extra laws and provides a continual new impulse that was attractive to new followers of a faith.

The disciples had been teaching what they knew from experience whereas Paul was teaching what he was receiving directly from Christ. That would have been viewed by unbelievers as similar to "New Age channeling" today. But it had vibrancy and, more importantly, Paul knew how to advise Gentiles living in Greek society with reference to their relationship with unbelievers; how to deal with fellow Christians who had fallen into temptation; the conduct of family life and the importance of accepting the teaching authority of the leaders of the new Church.

Much of what he writes is contradictory—and the authorship of several of his letters is questionable—but they were deeply valued by his followers.

As the original disciples died and direct contact with the physical Jesus faded, it was the written word that was trusted. That could be read out loud to a group of people again and again whereas telling a story verbally ran the risk of making it inaccurate.

Paul was also a master of spin. We've already looked at his very effective emotional blackmail in Chapter Three as he encouraged the people of Corinth to be generous with their donations towards his work. But in **2 Corinthians**, here he is again.

"I know your eagerness to help, and I have been boasting about it to the Macedonians, telling them that since last year you in Achaia were ready to give; and your enthusiasm has stirred most of them to action. But I am sending the brothers in order that our boasting about you in this matter should not prove hollow, but that you may be ready, as I said you would be. For if any Macedonians come with me and find you unprepared, we—not to say anything about you— would be ashamed of having been so confident." (**2 Cor 9:1-7**).

The love of money
Even so, our abiding memory of Paul's writings in the area of prosperity is the often misquoted *"Money is the root of all evil."*

That phrase on its own is seriously misrepresentative of Paul's message. The full quotation is this:

> *"But godliness with contentment is great gain. For we brought nothing into this world, and it is certain we can carry nothing out. And, having food and raiment, let us be therewith content. But they that will be rich fall into temptation and a snare, and into many foolish and hurtful lusts, which drown men in destruction and perdition. For the love of money is a root of all evil: which while some coveted after, they have erred from the faith, and pierced themselves through with many sorrows"* (**1 Tim 6:5**).

The Greek word translated as "love of money" is *philarguria* and it means avarice or greed and, as such, refers to the breaking of the tenth commandment *"Thou shalt not covet."* Paul is trying to make it clear, as Jesus did, that attaching to financial wealth over all other things is harmful to the soul. To do so is to make money a god which also breaks the first commandment.

But there is another important aspect of this quotation too. The word nearly always quoted as "evil" is mistranslated.

The word in Greek is *kakos*. The Greek word for evil, used everywhere else in the New Testament, is *poneros*. So Paul is saying, "Obsession over money is a (not 'the') root of all the crap in life."

As someone who was once so broke that I had to check my bank accounts every morning and sometimes walk a mile in order to take £5 out of one account and put it in another in order not to go over my overdraft limit, I can relate to that. And I expect you can too.

Paul does not say that money should be hated or despised — just not made the whole object of existence. People tend to think that *"having food and raiment, let us therewith content"* means that we should live with the minimum of comfort but that is not its correct translation. Again, it is vital to look at the Biblical meaning in the context of the time. Nobody in Paul's time had a mortgage nor gas and electricity bills — but if they had, the Greek word that is translated as "food" would cover all those. The word is *diatrophe* which means *a sufficient supply of that which nurtures and sustains us*. It's not just referring to enough to eat but all that we need to sustain a pleasing and nourishing life. In the modern world that word could perfectly well include holidays, a good car, a decent audio-visual system and regular pay rises.

Often I ask people if they would worry about money if they knew that there would never be any mortgage, rent or tax to pay, no bills, clothing came free and if they knew that they would always have all that they needed to eat and supply their home. The answer is always "no."

Paul says that "some" have erred from their faith through focusing on financial gain, not that *all* are prone to do so and it is true that focusing on money and money alone (whether through worry about lack of it or the wish to accumulate in order to justify their egos) is destructive. But it is not an injunction to endure poverty.

Later on in the same letter, Paul writes confidently again about the importance of giving by those who are wealthy so it would appear to be quite clear that he did not have issue with riches; just what we chose to do with them.

Conclusion

There is no possibility of encapsulating all the wisdom in the Bible in this one small book. However, hopefully you will have seen a pattern emerging in the teachings about prosperity in both the Hebrew and New Testaments.

I submit that they can be summed up as follows:

- Acknowledge, love and trust God, whatever your perception of God may be.

- Don't take on anyone else's version of God; you have to find your own path. Consider all spiritual teachings deeply, acknowledging the past but allowing them to be relevant to today.

- Honor the Holy One and the gift of your life by celebrating and enjoying God's gifts here on Earth.

- Take regular time out to allow yourself time to listen to God's word.

- Honor the land and release debts that cannot be paid to you.

- Understand that possessions are nice but not that important in the great scheme of things. If you can't let go of something you own in order to follow your dreams, then it's likely that the object possesses you rather than the other way round.

- Believe that if you ask, good will be given to you—but don't be attached to how it will come or in what exact form.

- Watch what you say and think about money or prosperity for *"life and death are in the power of the tongue"* (**Proverbs 18:21**)

- Don't make an enemy of money or those who have it; it is purely a means for exchange. It is what you do with it or think about it that makes it useful or harmful. You have a responsibility to use money for good.

- Give to others from the understanding of the above teachings so that you can pass on the wisdom of the ancients and help them to thrive too.

Bibliography

King James Bible with Strong's Hebrew and Greek Dictionary.

Accounting, Business & Financial History by Wayne A.M. Visser and Alastair McIntosh (Routledge).

Women and Religion in the First Christian Centuries, Deborah Sawyer (Routledge).

Financial Intermediation in the Early Roman Empire, Peter Temin (Social Science Research Network).

A History of the Jews, Paul Johnson. (HarperCollins).

Living in the Time of Jesus of Nazareth, Peter Connolly (Oxford University Press).

Misquoting Jesus, Prof. Bart Erhman (Harper One).

Testament, John Romer (Michael O'Mara Books).

Jesus & the Forgotten City: New Light on Sepphoris and the Urban World of Jesus. Richard A. Batey (Baker).

Wörterbuch über Talmudim und Midrachim, Yacob Levy, Berlin 1924.

Bible Background Commentary, C. S. Keener (IVP Academic).

Birth of Jesus, B. Witherington (DJG).

Rabbi Jesus, Bruce Chilton (Image).

Companion Bible, E. W. Bullinger (Kregel Publications).

The Jewish War, Flavius Josephus (Penguin).

The Secret, Rhonda Byrne (Simon & Schuster)

The Game of Life and How to Play It, Florence Scovell Shinn (De Vorss).

Prosperity, Charles Fillmore (Unity Classic Library).

The Millionaires of the Bible Series, Catherine Ponder (De Vorss).

Science & Health With Key to the Scriptures Mary Baker Eddy (M. B. Eddy).

AXIS MUNDI
BOOKS

Axis Mundi Books, provide the most revealing and coherent explorations and investigations of the world of hidden or forbidden knowledge. Take a fascinating journey into the realm of Esoteric Mysteries, Magic, Mysticism, Angels, Cosmology, Alchemy, Gnosticism, Theosophy, Kabbalah, Secret Societies and Religions, Symbolism, Quantum Theory, Apocalyptic Mythology, Holy Grail and Alternative Views of Mainstream Religion.